Engineering Wonders

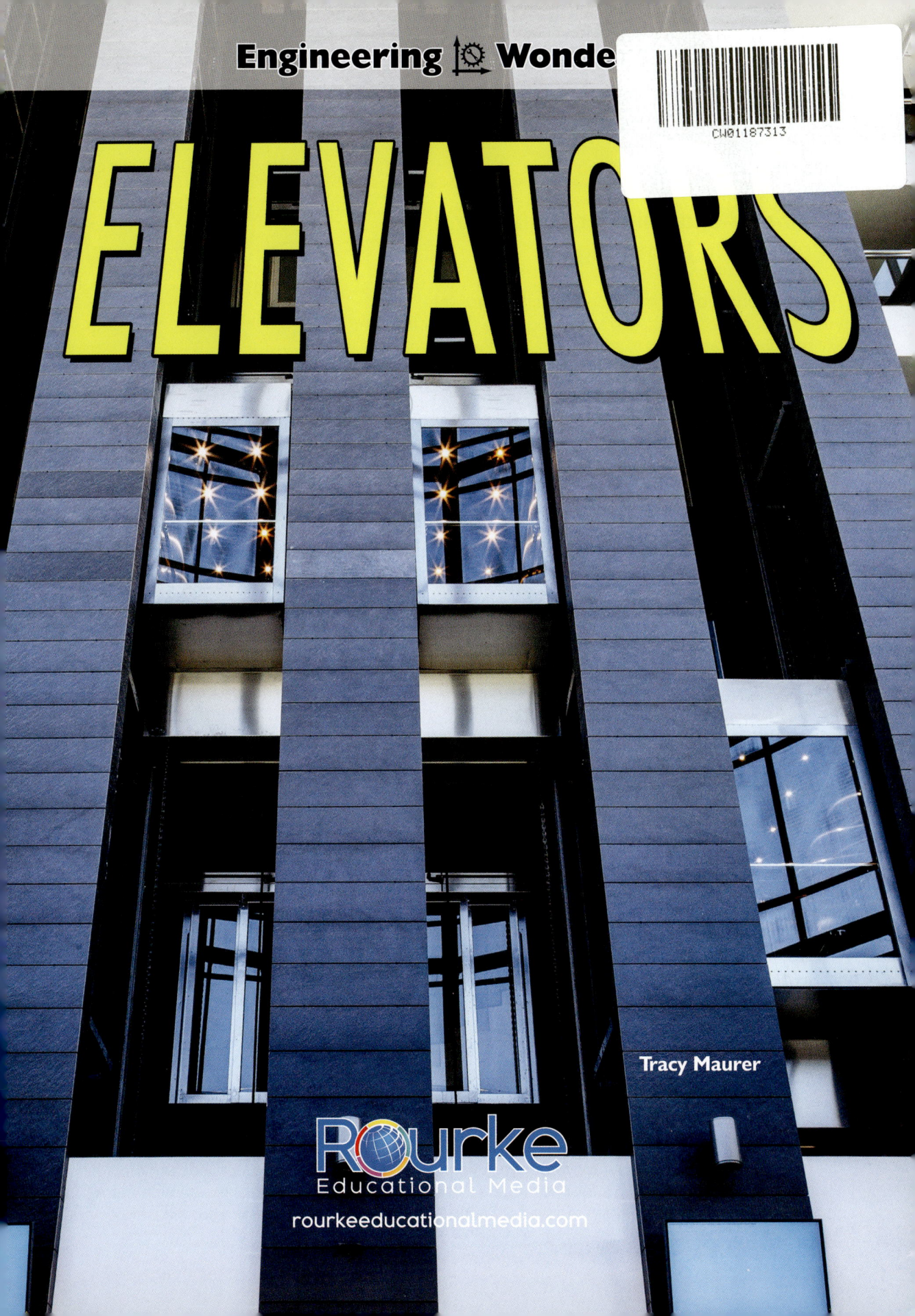

ELEVATORS

Tracy Maurer

Rourke
Educational Media

rourkeeducationalmedia.com

Before & After Reading Activities

Before Reading:

Building Academic Vocabulary and Background Knowledge

Before reading a book, it is important to tap into what your child or students already know about the topic. This will help them develop their vocabulary, increase their reading comprehension, and make connections across the curriculum.

1. Look at the cover of the book. What will this book be about?
2. What do you already know about the topic?
3. Let's study the Table of Contents. What will you learn about in the book's chapters?
4. What would you like to learn about this topic? Do you think you might learn about it from this book? Why or why not?
5. Use a reading journal to write about your knowledge of this topic. Record what you already know about the topic and what you hope to learn about the topic.
6. Read the book.
7. In your reading journal, record what you learned about the topic and your response to the book.
8. After reading the book complete the activities below.

Content Area Vocabulary
Read the list. What do these words mean?

counterweight
hangar bay
hydraulic
inspections
observation deck
pressure
pulley
residential
tenants

After Reading:

Comprehension and Extension Activity

After reading the book, work on the following questions with your child or students in order to check their level of reading comprehension and content mastery.

1. How does a building's use affect elevator design? (Asking Questions)
2. What factors need to be considered when designing an elevator? (Summarize)
3. Why is it important for elevators to move people quickly? (Infer)
4. What are some safety features in modern elevators? (Summarize)
5. Have you ridden in an elevator in a tall building? How tall was it? What do you remember about the experience? Share your thoughts about it. (Text to Self Connection)

Extension Activity

Engineers carefully plan elevators for pleasant passenger experiences. Wash out a milk carton. Cut open one side. This is your elevator cab. Decide what type of building it services and how far it will need to travel. Decorate it for passengers. What would make an elevator experience more comfortable or more memorable? Add safety features. Share your design with your classmates and family. Explain your choices.

TABLE OF CONTENTS

Lifting Up, Lowering Down 4
Ancient Elevators 8
Otis Changes Skylines 14
From Landmarks to Sailing Ships 20
Other Lifting Machines 26
Modern Elevators 30
Reaching New Heights 42
Timeline 45
Glossary 46
Index 47
Show What You Know 47
Websites to Visit 47
About the Author 48

LIFTING UP, LOWERING DOWN

How do you move people, animals, and materials to different heights and down again—safely and quickly? Ancient humans made ladders, carved handholds, and built steep stairways into rock walls. An elevator would have been helpful.

The Sinagua people built cliff homes in the 13th and 14th centuries where Arizona is today.

No one knows when early engineers first tackled this challenge. Sometime after the wheel was invented, they discovered the **pulley**.

This well uses a type of fixed pulley.

A pulley is a simple machine that uses a long pulling rope with a load attached on one end. The other end is threaded along a grooved wheel. The wheel changes the direction of the pull.

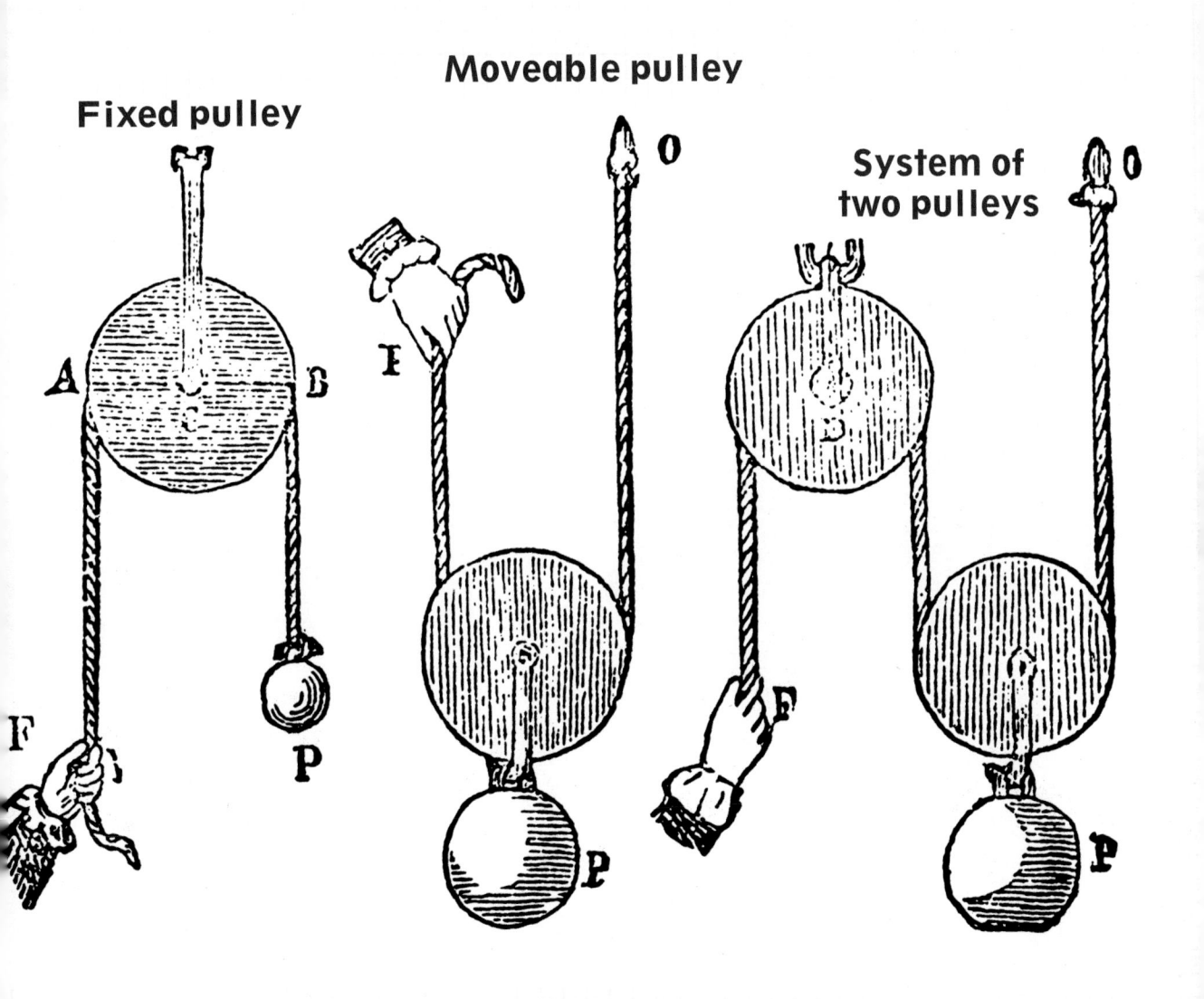

Fixed pulley

Moveable pulley

System of two pulleys

ANCIENT ELEVATORS

How did ancient Egyptians lift heavy stone to build pyramids some 4,600 years ago? They had no iron to make a strong pulley axle. Researchers think ancient Egyptians used a polished stone cylinder with a groove carved for a rope. The cylinder could turn smoothly in a stone cradle as workers pulled the rope.

Math at Work
The Greek scholar Archimedes developed an elevator around 236 BCE. It used a screw to lift water for crops.

Each block in the Great Pyramid of Giza, in Egypt, weighs about 5,000 pounds (2,268 kilograms).

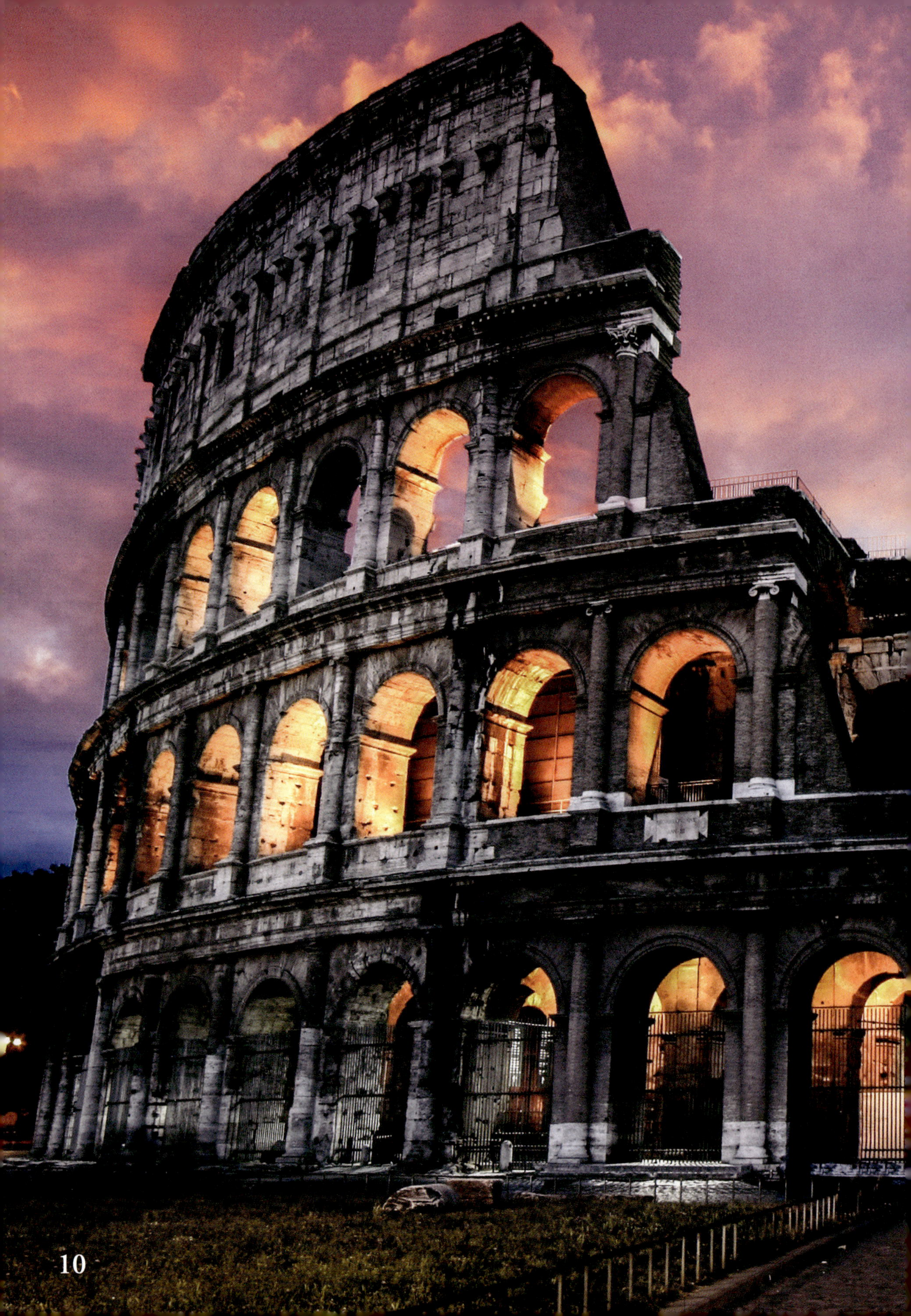

Ancient Romans used pulleys in a system of elevators and trap doors in their Colosseum. Hundreds of men powered the elevators. They lifted people, animals, and ships from underground staging areas to the Colosseum floor.

The Colosseum was built between 70 and 80 CE.

At first, elevators were powered by people, animals, or water. Steam power came with the Industrial Revolution around 1760.

Early steam-powered elevators were attached to a cylinder. The cylinder fit inside a shaft. This shaft was as deep underground as the building was tall. Adding steam **pressure** under the cylinder slowly raised the elevator. Releasing the pressure lowered the elevator—not always so slowly!

This drawing shows an early steam engine system used only for elevators.

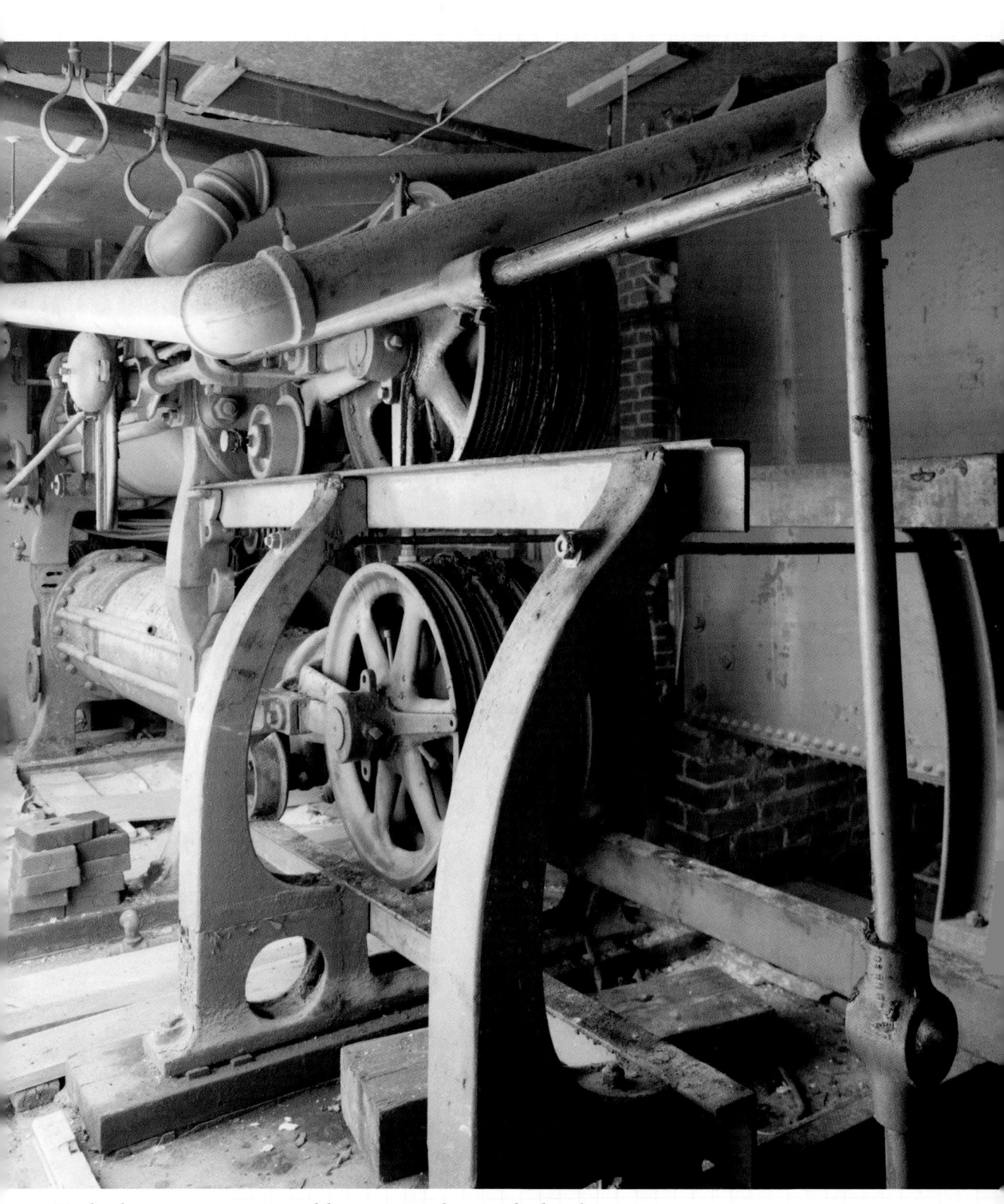

Early elevators were powered by steam and water hydraulic pistons.

OTIS CHANGES SKYLINES

In 1854, Elisha Otis (1811–1861) introduced a new steam-powered freight elevator with a safety brake in London. To prove it worked, he rode his elevator up. Then his assistant cut the rope. The gathered crowd gasped. People thought he would crash.

Soon, cheaper **hydraulic** systems replaced steam power. Elevators could reach higher and faster. Buildings grew taller. Skylines changed forever.

Hydraulic systems use fluid power to do simple work.

Many people felt uneasy in elevators. Engineers developed systems so the cab door opened level with the building floor. They added escape hatches and emergency telephones. Soft music also comforted passengers.

Elevator companies designed their cabs to look like fancy rooms.

16

Women Take Control
Operating an elevator became one of the first "acceptable" jobs for women in the late 1800s. Operators controlled how fast the cab traveled and where it stopped.

17

In 1889, Elisha Otis's son Norton (1840–1905) added an electric motor to control the cable. He also connected the cab to a **counterweight**. This reduced the power needed to lift the cab.

A counterweight usually equals the weight of the elevator car plus 40 percent of the greatest load it can carry.

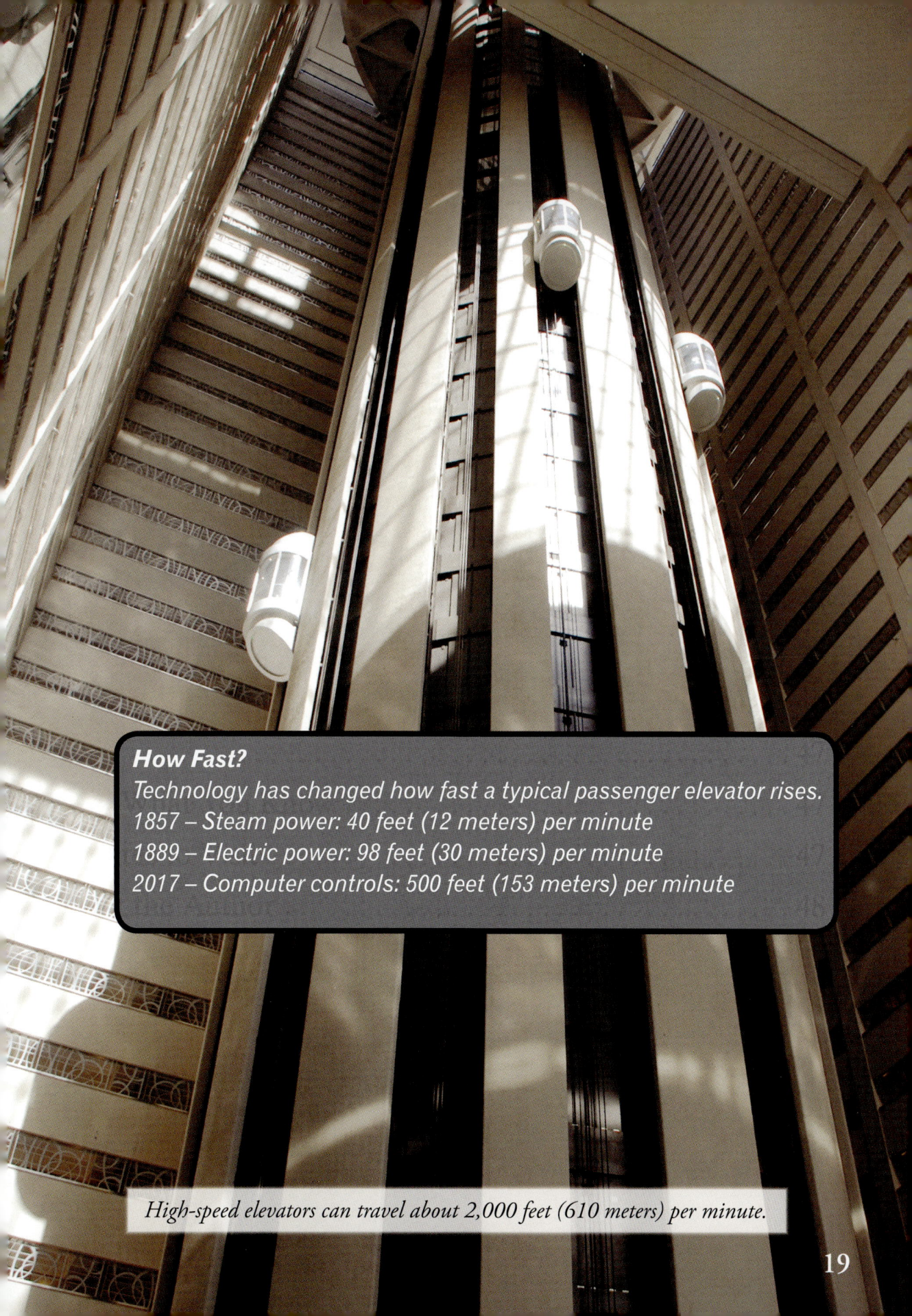

How Fast?
Technology has changed how fast a typical passenger elevator rises.
1857 – Steam power: 40 feet (12 meters) per minute
1889 – Electric power: 98 feet (30 meters) per minute
2017 – Computer controls: 500 feet (153 meters) per minute

High-speed elevators can travel about 2,000 feet (610 meters) per minute.

FROM LANDMARKS TO SAILING SHIPS

To add elevator shafts to designs, architects must think about:
- building use
- carrying loads
- cab size
- power source
- system weight
- travel speed
- height and size of the shaft
- cost of materials
- location in the building
- safety

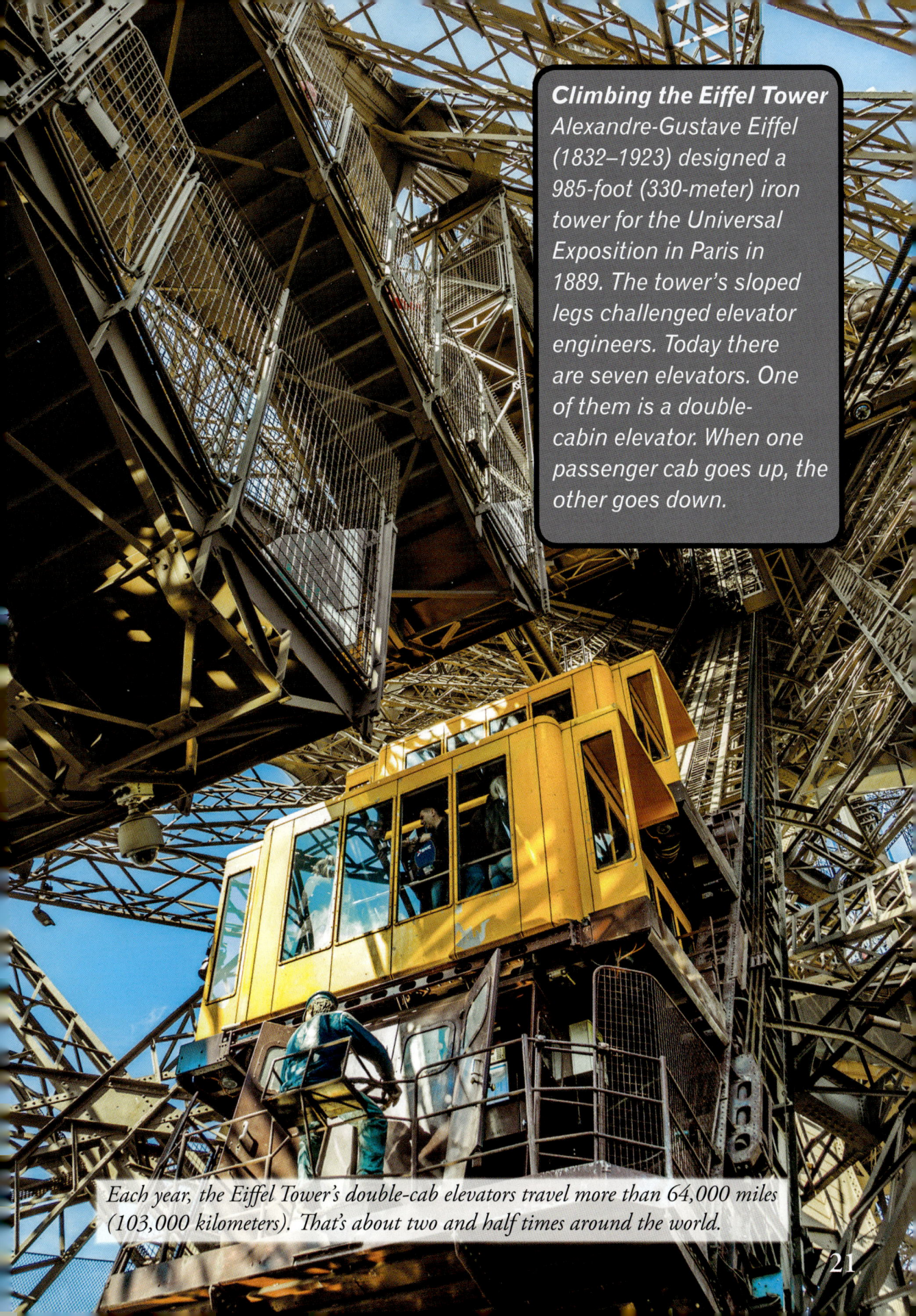

Climbing the Eiffel Tower
Alexandre-Gustave Eiffel (1832–1923) designed a 985-foot (330-meter) iron tower for the Universal Exposition in Paris in 1889. The tower's sloped legs challenged elevator engineers. Today there are seven elevators. One of them is a double-cabin elevator. When one passenger cab goes up, the other goes down.

Each year, the Eiffel Tower's double-cab elevators travel more than 64,000 miles (103,000 kilometers). That's about two and half times around the world.

Landmark buildings challenge engineers to build elevators for large numbers of tourists.

The CN Tower in Toronto, Canada, features the world's highest glass-floor elevators. Tourists can look straight down 1,136 feet (346 meters).

22

When it opened in 1932, the Empire State Building in New York City was the world's tallest building at 1,250 feet (381 meters). Its 73 elevators carry about 200 people per hour. Tourists still wait in long lines to reach the **observation deck**.

Some elevators bring tourists underground. Hoover Dam between Arizona and Nevada opened in 1936. In the 1990s, a new elevator was added to handle more tourists. A special drill carefully bored a shaft 572 feet (174 meters) deep.

A 70-second elevator ride brings visitors to the lower lobby of Hoover Dam.

Computers control the massive elevators on aircraft carriers.

Elevators at Sea
The **hangar bay** on an aircraft carrier stores about 60 aircraft and gear two levels below the flight deck. Huge hydraulic platform elevators can each lift two 74,000-pound (33,566 kilogram) fighter jets.

25

OTHER LIFTING MACHINES

Other lifting solutions include the **escalator**. It keeps moving in a loop. No one waits long for a ride. Ski lifts also travel in loops using pulleys.

Handrails loop at the same speed as stairs.

Slots on tracks keep stairs level.

Two pairs of looped chains move stairs.

North America's longest escalator is at the Wheaton Metro stop in Washington, D.C. It spans 230 feet (70 meters). That's about the length of six school buses!

Cranes and hoists are common lifting machines at construction sites. Tower cranes with long booms use a pulley system and a rear counterweight.

The Aerial Lift Bridge in Duluth, Minnesota, lifts only the bridge deck. It works like an elevator. It has large counterweights to raise the deck 135 feet (41 meters).

MODERN ELEVATORS

Elevators have changed city skylines. Without elevators, there would be no skyscrapers. In a tall structure, the building's core houses the elevator shafts.

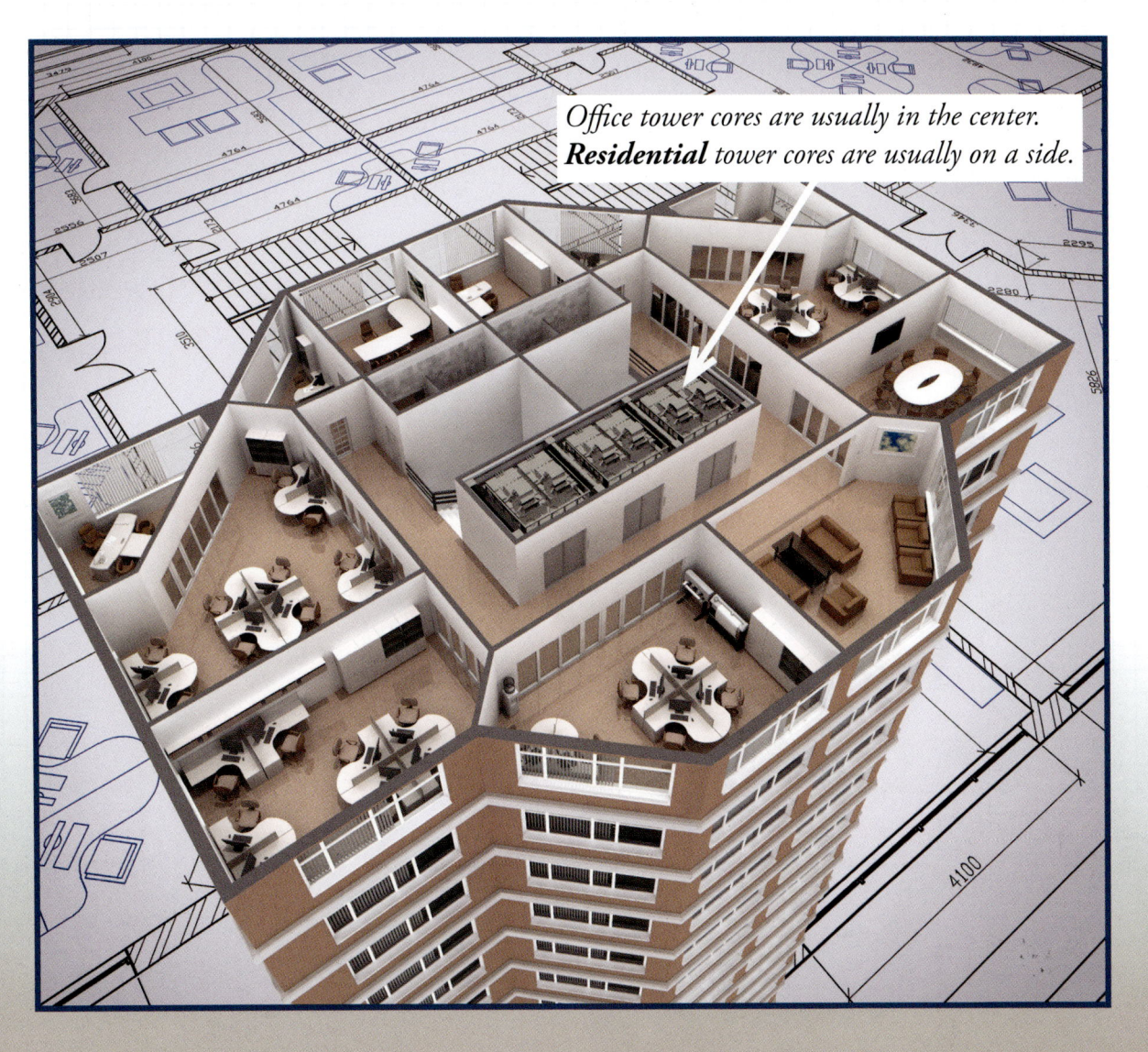

Office tower cores are usually in the center. ***Residential*** *tower cores are usually on a side.*

Offices hold more people than homes or hotels. Elevators in these buildings are used most often during work hours. Residents and hotel guests use elevators day and night. They use elevators less often than office workers do.

More than 325 million riders use an elevator each day.

If a building has both office and residential **tenants**, two elevators may serve the residential floors. Additional elevators will serve the busy office floors.

Elevators are expensive to install and operate. They also take up floor space that building owners can sell. Building owners install the fewest number of elevators needed to keep wait times short. Eight elevators can handle a building 15 to 20 stories tall.

Elevator installers and repair technicians must use extreme caution to avoid injury on the job. There are many risks involoved when working on an elevator.

Elevators in the United States make 18 billion passenger trips per year.

35

Modern skyscrapers make the most of their elevator space. Double-deck elevators load and unload at two floors at the same time. Elevators in super-tall buildings speed up and down to move people quickly. This can affect the air pressure. Some elevators use air pressure systems to keep passengers' ears from popping.

The Taipei 101 building in Taiwan has one of the world's fastest elevators. It reaches the 101st floor in 39 seconds.

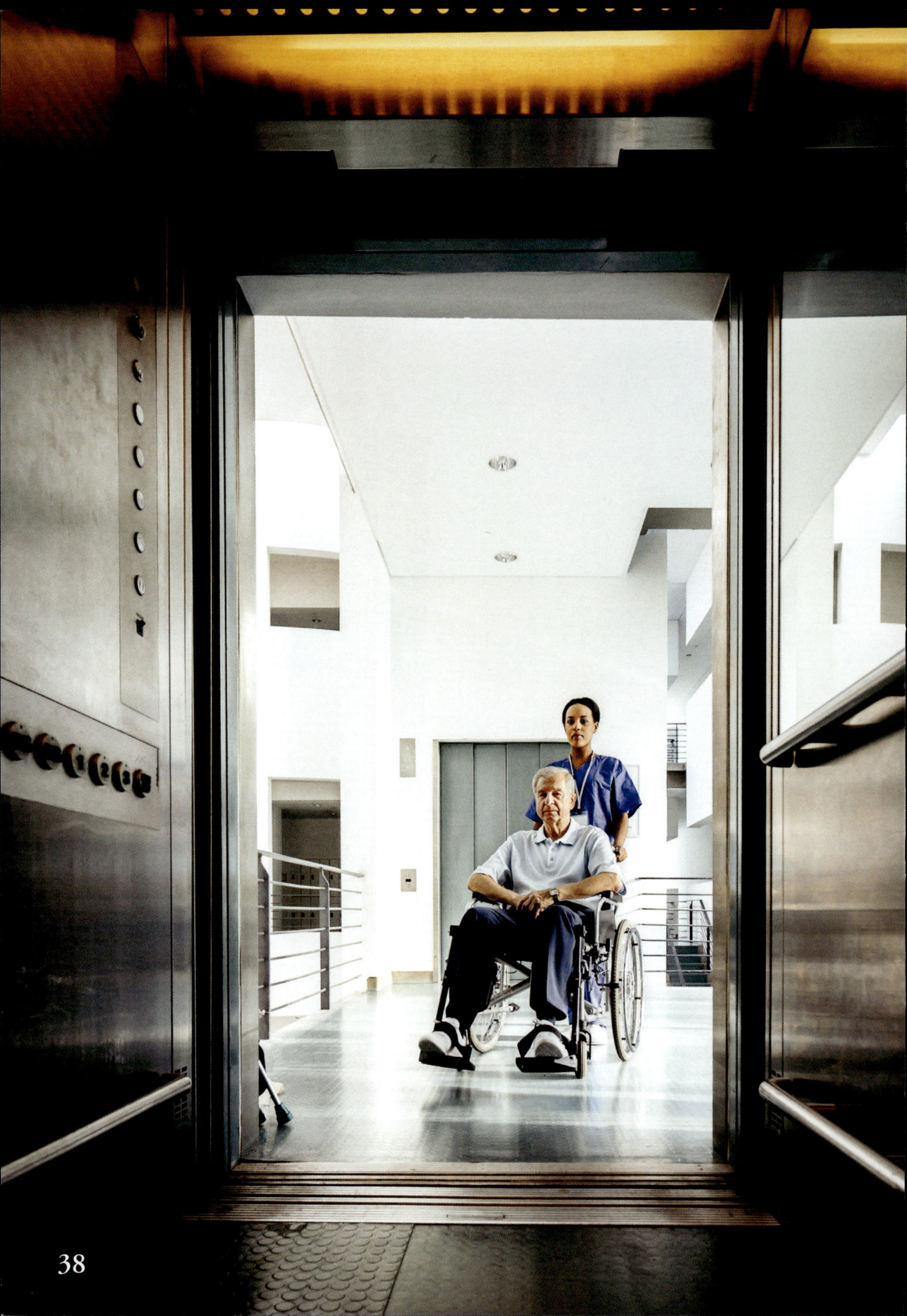

In the United States, elevators must meet safety standards and pass **inspections**. Elevators must be safe for people in wheelchairs. They must also have safety features for people with sight and hearing impairments.

People in wheelchairs use elevators every day.

Skyscrapers with observation decks for tourists have the largest elevators. These shuttles can carry more than 40 passengers at one time.

Time Travel
The One World Observatory at One World Trade Center in New York City uses video panels to show how the city has changed over the past 500 years.

One World Trade Center has 71 elevators. Five are high-speed shuttles that travel to the 101st floor in 47 seconds.

Buildings must have freight elevators to service the loading dock. They are usually larger and taller than passenger elevators. Some countries also require firefighter lifts.

Firefighters often use a special switch to control an elevator in an emergency.

41

REACHING NEW HEIGHTS

Technology allows engineers to design taller, faster, and safer elevators. Computers control the cabs and their safety systems. Lasers can scan floors for passengers and send an elevator where it's needed.

Companies work to improve elevator designs. Someday, elevator systems may not even use cables.

Modern elevators use energy wisely. Some systems even use motors that turn braking power into electricity.

Mile-High Marvel
Architects have drawn plans for a Tokyo skyscraper one mile (1.6 kilometers) high. It's scheduled to open in 2045.

Elevator designs are becoming common for homes, schools, and other buildings with only two levels. As always, people need vertical transportation. Elevators are the engineering wonders that move us up and down safely and easily.

TIMELINE

Prehistoric times – An engineer invents the pulley.

2649-2150 BCE – Egyptians build the Great Pyramid of Giza.

236 BCE – Archimedes designs a screw-based lift.

70 CE – Romans build the Colosseum.

1760 – Industrial Revolution begins.

1854 – Elisha Otis introduces a safety elevator.

1889 – Norton Otis adds an electric motor and counterweight.

1889 – The Eiffel Tower opens in Paris.

1932 – Empire State Building opens.

1936 – Hoover Dam opens.

2013 – Researchers reconstruct ancient Egyptian pulley system.

2014 – One World Observatory in One World Trade Center opens.

2045 – Sky Mile Tower scheduled to open in Japan.

GLOSSARY

counterweight (KOUN-tur-wate): a heavy support on the weak side to help balance a load

hangar bay (HANG-ur BAY): a place where aircraft are stored or repaired

hydraulic (hye-DRAW-lik): moving water or other liquid in pipes under pressure to make power

inspections (in-SPEK-shuhns): close observations of something

observation deck (ahb-zur-VAY-shuhn DEK): a place set aside for viewing a city or other scenery

pressure (PRESH-ur): force made by pressing something

pulley (PUL-ee): a lifting machine made from rope or chain and a grooved wheel

residential (rezi-DEN-shuhl): having to do with an area where people live

tenants (TEN-uhnts): people or businesses that rent a place that belongs to someone else

INDEX

Colosseum 11
counterweight(s) 18, 28, 29
Egyptians 8
Eiffel Tower 21
escalator 26, 27
hangar bay 25
hydrolic 15, 25
observation deck(s) 23, 40
Otis, Elisha 14, 18
pressure 12, 36
pulley(s) 6, 7, 8, 11, 26, 28
residential 31, 33
Romans 11

SHOW WHAT YOU KNOW

1. What are common safety features in modern elevators?
2. Who developed the first safety steam-powered elevator?
3. How have elevators changed city skylines?
4. How are elevators different in office buildings compared to residential buildings?
5. In addition to elevators, what else uses a pulley system?

WEBSITES TO VISIT

http://science.howstuffworks.com/transport/engines-equipment/elevator.htm
www.madehow.com/Volume-2/Elevator.html
http://discoverykids.com/articles/how-do-elevators-work

ABOUT THE AUTHOR

Tracy Maurer has written more than 100 books for young readers. She holds an MFA in writing for children and young adults from Hamline University. Her home is near Minneapolis, a busy city with many tall buildings thanks to elevators.

Meet The Author!
www.meetREMauthors.com

© 2018 Rourke Educational Media

All rights reserved. No part of this book may be reproduced or utilized in any form or by any means, electronic or mechanical including photocopying, recording, or by any information storage and retrieval system without permission in writing from the publisher.

www.rourkeeducationalmedia.com

PHOTO CREDITS: Cover and title page: ©Unbekannt; p.5: ©DCorn; p.6: ©Tramino; p.7, 8: ©ilbusca; p.8, 43: Wiki; p.9: ©Karim Hesham; p.10-11: ©Bryan_Redding; p.12: ©Science History Images/Alamy Stock Photo; p.13, 15, 16, 17: Courtesy of Library of Congress; p.14: ©Corbis; p.18: ©Chronicle/Alamy Stock Photo; p.19: ©Yulia1Dreamstime.com; p.20: ©Serge_Bertasius; p.21: ©Meinzahn; p.22: ©Alessandro Lai, ©Kay Roxby/Alamy Stock Photo; p.23: ©frankysze, ©Maciej Bledowski/Alamy Stock Photo; p.24: ©tupungato, ©Radharc Images/Alamy Stock Photo; p.25: Courtesy of United States Navy; p.26: ©huad262; p.27: ©eternalsphere25; p.28: ©james steidl; p.29: ©Jenny Swanson; p.30-31: ©bluejayphoto; p.31: ©nikonaft; p.32: ©lovro77; p.33: ©charles taylor, ©travelpixpro; p.34: ©alacatr; p.35: ©kruwt; p.36: ©Marcel Lam Photography; p.37: ©GoranQ; p.38: ©TommL; p.39: ©aozora1, ©Jaren Jai Wicklund; p.40: ©Victoria Lipov, ©Sainaniritu/Dreamstime.com; p.41: ©muzafferakarca, ©Corey Sundahl; p.42: ©Nico Pudimat Fotografic

Edited by: Keli Sipperley
Cover and interior design by: Rhea Magaro-Wallace

Library of Congress PCN Data

Elevators / Tracy Maurer
(Engineering Wonders)
ISBN 978-1-68342-392-8 (hard cover)(alk.paper)
ISBN 978-1-68342-462-8 (soft cover)
ISBN 978-1-68342-558-8 (e-Book)
Library of Congress Control Number: 2017931284

Rourke Educational Media
Printed in the United States of America, North Mankato, Minnesota